MW00627169

# THINK SMALL

**A Millennial's Guide to Building a Meaningful Life
in Rural America**

Matthew Hoagland

24 August 2020

Copyright © 2020 Matthew Hoagland
Written by Matthew Hoagland

All rights reserved. No portion of this book may be repro-
duced in any form or by any electronic or mechanical means
including information storage and retrieval systems – except
in the case of brief quotations embodied in critical articles or
reviews – without permission in writing from Matthew Hoagland.

This book depicts real events in the life of the author as honestly as memory permits. The author's successful transition
from an urban to a rural lifestyle provides no assurances of
similar success should the reader follow the tips, sugges-
tions, guidance and/or advice provided in this book.

Published by Matthew Hoagland
Yanceyville, NC
www.HowToThinkSmall.com

This book is published in association with:
Lea Street Press, LLC, Blanch, NC
LeaStreetPress.com
LeaStreetPress@gmail.com

Issued in print and electronic formats.
Paperback ISBN 978-1-7352470-0-7
E-book ISBN 978-1-7352470-1-4


Library of Congress Control Number: 2020911026

*Dedicated to my beautiful wife Celia
and our precious daughter Waylen.*

# Contents

# Introduction

This book will be light on statistics and heavy on anecdotes. This is my personal story...at least as best I remember it, especially the quotes. Though the chapters in this book will mostly retell my and my wife's story they are meant to be a general guide for how young professionals can move to and, for lack of a better term, conquer life in rural America.

The audience for this book is the frustrated reader in their twenties and thirties, those who may have a college degree, a drive to succeed, and maybe even an itch to explore a creative or entrepreneurial outlet but feel stuck. Maybe they grew up in one of America's most populated cities, or maybe they moved there after college. Now they find themselves in a profession that doesn't match their degree, saddled with a heaping amount of student loan debt, and a job that pays enough to cover rent and a weekend out with friends but makes them feel replaceable and unappreciated. Neither their job nor their community make them feel like they're part of something meaningful.

In the aftermath of COVID-19, they're wondering if life in such a crowded place is even worth it. Their solution may be to move to a small town they've never heard of and start over with a much lower cost of living, a much broader set of opportunities and a new chance to build a meaningful life.

I certainly believe it is because I've done it.

After graduating college in 2010, I lived in Asheville, North Carolina—a city of about ninety thousand people in a metro area of about four hundred thousand. My first rental was a room in big house that was walking distance to downtown and one of the best Jamaican restaurants in the world. City life was great. But along with all the fond memories, I also remember nauseating traffic jams and constant panhandling. My rental house was cool, but the fact that I shared a bathroom and kitchen with seven other housemates was not. It was all I could afford, and the high cost of living meant I had very little left over at the end of each month.

After a few years in Asheville, however, my wife and I transitioned to a small town that's about as opposite of big city life as it gets. And I couldn't be more thankful that we did. It drastically improved our lives.

The steps I took can be replicated, or at least borrowed from, in thousands of small communities across our country. This is the story of how we moved to a town I'd never heard of before, found rental property for cheap, got married for half the average cost, started a successful business, bought a house for $39,000, and how I landed one of the most high-profile jobs in town.

Your story will undoubtedly be different if you choose a similar path to mine. But if you're willing to ask tough questions, learn new things, and work hard toward your goals, then you can not only carve out a great life for yourself in rural America, but also quickly become one of the most well-known and influential people in your community. Heck, you might even develop some of the most genuine friendships you've ever had. We certainly did. Before you know it, you'll have an impact on your new community that's much larger than the one you had by blending into the crowd of a bigger city.

As you get started, please keep the following in mind. I have written this book in a way that makes it possible for you to finish it in one week. Who has time for a long book anyway? Seven chapters—one per day—and you'll have it finished in no time. Then use it to make your own small-town search, to-do lists, and year-to-year plans. I've even included some handy checklists in the back to get you started. Let a friend borrow it and encourage them to do the same. Hang on to it as you make your move to Small Town, USA. Consult it from time to time as you get involved, apply for jobs, start a business, buy a house, get married, or embark on any similar adventure. Use any or all of it to start your story today.

Here's my story and how I did it.

# Chapter 1
## How to Move to "The Middle of Nowhere"

It was June or July of 2015; I don't remember exactly. My girlfriend and I sat at a table in one of our favorite restaurants, The Local Joint in Fairview, North Carolina, a small community just ten miles southeast of the famously quirky Asheville. We'd lived there for the last couple of years. After college, I found a well-paying recruiting job in south Asheville and Celia had just finished her master's degree in Sustainability Studies at Lenoir-Rhyne University. We had a network of great friends. Our free time was spent at craft breweries, trendy restaurants, and bohemian street festivals.

"I really want to move to Yanceyville soon," Celia told me, "to be closer to my family and the horses. And I'm thinking like the end of this year."

"I don't think I am ready for that," I hesitantly responded and tried to explain. I could see tears begin to well in her eyes.

Celia grew up in Greensboro, North Carolina. However, once she and her brothers had all gone off to college or moved out, her parents started looking for a property with a house and enough acreage for their horses. For years, they'd been renting a barn about thirty minutes away, making daily feeding and caring for the animals a time-consuming task. Then in 2013 they found the right property in Caswell County, North Carolina, just outside the county seat of Yanceyville, a town of just over two thousand residents. I had never even heard of the place until their search led them to the far reaches of the metro area.

She had thought about how to have this conversation with me, I could tell. Though we were simply boyfriend and girlfriend now, I had already begun plans to buy a ring and propose marriage in just a few months. We hadn't really talked about that either, at least not in great detail.

Then a million other thoughts raced through my head. Didn't we want to settle down in Asheville? I was a native of Western North Carolina, and she knew how much I loved the mountains and the culture of the area...not to mention that a lot of my family were nearby. Plus, a lot of my old college buddies were there. I had a good job; I couldn't just up and leave it. Where would I work in one of the most rural counties in the state? What would it be like to live somewhere so remarkably different? I had even thought about one day running for public office in the Asheville area. That would require years of establishing deep roots in the community. I'd have to kiss that idea goodbye for sure.

"Well when do you think you might be ready?" she asked.

"I don't know...maybe a year, year and a half..." I responded. The idea of moving so soon just shocked my system. I always knew we'd have to think seriously about it someday, especially if we wanted to get married, but I didn't expect us to have the conversation so soon. Maybe if I had a year or so to prepare it would be easier.

It was a tough, tense conversation. She cried as we talked...and I hate to see her cry.

Our lunch ended awkwardly but in the next few days things began to settle down. We got back into our daily routines after the weekend and had more conversations about what the move might actually look like. No tears this time. We had already planned for a cross-country road trip in September, and I needed to broach that conversation with my boss soon if we wanted to start solidifying plans and ensure we had the time off to do it. To me, it made sense to go ahead and make the two big requests at the same time. I'm a big "rip the bandage off now" kind of guy.

I envisioned myself saying, "Hey boss, I need a month off work to go on a cross country adventure and oh, by the way, I'm thinking of moving four hours away in a few months. Is that cool and can I keep my job?"

Looking back, it sounds crazy. But Tim, my boss, was a pretty cool guy. He actually encouraged his employees to have these kinds of life experiences, as long as it didn't interfere with our work, of course. Recruiting is primarily an over-the-phone sales job that involves finding qualified candidates for hard-to-fill positions in other companies. So as long as my annual sales up to that point were solid—and I could convince him my job performance would stay strong through the move—I felt pretty good about him granting me both requests.

It must have been a day or two after that, a normal day at the office, when the conversation occurred. It was a little after five o'clock on a Wednesday, I think. All my coworkers had left for the day and the lights were off in the building except for the ones over Tim's desk. I figured it was now or never, so I mustered up the courage to approach him with my plans.

"Hey boss man," I said with a mixture of nervousness and excitement, "I've got a couple big questions to ask you."

"Sure thing, what's up?" he asked. So I began to lay it all out there. First, was the road trip. He was immediately interested and asked all about the national parks and states we planned to visit. He even shared some stories of trips he'd taken in the past. I then let him know that I planned to pop the question to Celia during our trip. He was understandably very excited to be let in on the secret. I'm pretty sure he texted his wife the news before I could even finish the sentence.

"Well, it sounds like a fun trip and you've brought in some good revenue this year," he said. "So go ahead and take September for your road trip. But don't make a habit of taking this much time off. This is a one-time reward for your work at the firm. And I am excited you two will be getting married. Now what's your next question?"

"Celia wants us to move to Yanceyville," I said with a wince.

"Where the hell is Yanceyville?" he asked. "Is that in North Carolina?"

"Yep," I said. "It's kind of north of Greensboro, right on the Virginia line." He sat up in his computer chair and entered the location into Google to find it on the map.

"Dude, that's in the middle of nowhere." "Why do y'all want to move there?"

"She wants to be closer to her family and their horses," I responded. "Ya know...her family has like ten horses, and her parents are getting older...they're gonna need help managing their farm in the next few years, and she wants to be there for that."

"So does this mean you're quitting the firm?"

"No! I definitely don't want to do that," I assured him. "I'm hoping there's a way we could set up a computer and a phone so I can work remotely."

"You mean like work from home?" he asked.

"Well...not exactly, I think I'll get a little stir crazy if I'm at home all day. I need a change of scenery, ya know?"

"So what about setting up an office at her parents' farm?" he countered.

"Well maybe…but I think I'd still go a little stir-crazy just sitting at their place all day. What if I was able to find a remote office for really cheap? Is that something you think we could manage?" I asked.

He thought for a second. "I tell you what…if you can find an office for a really low price and bring in enough revenue to pay for itself, then I think we can make a deal. But I'm gonna be watching your numbers. This is not something I like to do and we already have two guys working remotely. If I'm not careful, everyone here will be thinking they can work from home."

I assured him I could make it work. And I knew that if I did enough leg work between now and the end of the year then I could find a place with cheap rent close to town. I mean, how much could it possibly cost to rent a decent office in such a small market, right? My goal would be to have a place lined up and ready for work by January 2016, once the Christmas break was over. Celia and I had agreed that January 1, 2016 would be a good move-in day and would make it easier to get out of our current rental agreement and into a new one.

"Well I'll be sorry to see you go, Hoagland," Tim told me. "We love having you here at the office but this is how life goes sometimes. Just try to come back and visit us whenever you can."

I left work just before six o'clock that night after my talk with Tim. My challenge lay before me. It was time to buckle down and do some research. Not only did we have to plan for a cross-country road trip that would take us ten thousand miles across America, but we had to find a place to live, and I had to find an office to rent that would justify the cost for my boss. Oh yeah...I was also on the cusp of buying an engagement ring and popping the question to my future wife. It was crunch time on some major decisions that were guaranteed to shape the rest of my life.

I got home from work and shared the news with Celia. We were both excited to start making our future plans right away. Our first item of business was planning the September road trip. As I mentioned, our adventures covered ten thousand miles and included stops in nearly half the states in the country, breathtaking hikes in national parks, camping in state parks, a dozen state capitol building tours, four-wheeling up the sand dunes of the Oregon coast and—oh yeah—a marriage proposal to Celia at the foot of Avalanche Lake in Glacier National Park.

It was life changing. If you ever get the chance to travel our country—engagement or not—definitely do it. It's amazing. I could go on and on about the beauty and wonder of it all, but perhaps those stories will wait for another book.

Back home in Asheville, it was time to start planning for what was next. I had three months to find a house and an office to rent in a town where I knew basically no one. How the hell was I going to pull this off?

# Chapter 2
## How to Find Cheap Places to Rent

Since college, looking for a place to rent had always been easy. Step one: go online and search. Step two: contact the owners or management company to stop in and see the place. Step three: sign a lease or don't. This is pretty much how it works in any college town or big city, but that was not the case as I started looking in and around Yanceyville.

I started with looking for a place to live. That was clearly the most important. Even if I couldn't find an office, we needed a house, and worst-case scenario, I could just work from home even if it made me stir-crazy. So, I started with Craigslist. I pulled up the website and sorted by city. Danville, Virginia is geographically the closest city to Yanceyville that's listed. It's a city of just about forty-five thousand residents. I perused the rental options for a minute but didn't see anything promising. Too much to sift through. So I tried to 10narrow the options by keying in "Yanceyville" in the search bar. No results.

"What the hell?" I thought. "That's odd."

I tried broadening the search to Caswell County. One result: a busted up mobile home way off in the woods somewhere at the end of a gravel road. That would definitely *not* work.

So I thought for a second. Caswell is in North Carolina after all and sometimes lumped in with the Greensboro/Triad region (the area consisting of Greensboro, High Point, Winston-Salem and their surrounding counties). Maybe I should approach this from that angle instead. I backed out of my search criteria and retried all the same steps but this time through the Greensboro portal. Again, nothing. "This is insane!" I thought to myself. How the hell were there literally no rental options in this place? I'd scoured real estate websites before and found plenty of listings I thought were either too expensive or in a bad location, but nothing? What was I getting myself into?

I looked on Zillow but discovered basically the same results. I checked some local real estate agency websites in Danville, but all their rentals were over the state line in Virginia. Maybe that was our best bet. Maybe we should settle for becoming Virginia residents and find a place there. But my irrational pride in being a North Carolinian just would not let me do that.

I found the one and only real estate agent in Caswell County and gave her a call. Her company's website showed only homes for sale but that couldn't be all there was. Plus, if anyone would know about available rental properties it would be this lady. She was the only game in town! My call to her office went unanswered and I had to leave a voicemail. A couple of days passed and still no return call. So I called again and left yet another voicemail explaining who we were and what we were looking for. Still no return call that day or the next. I couldn't believe this.

I started imagining ulterior motives. Maybe they didn't want a couple of hipster kids moving into their small town from big city Asheville. Maybe they didn't want any "outsiders" at all. I bet was because we were living together but not married yet. You know how traditional these places can be, right?

I finally give up and handed the information over to Celia. I told her about my failed attempts to call and thought maybe she'd have better luck. She was actually headed out to stay with her parents that weekend and was going to try to stop by the real estate office if possible.

It must have been the next day. Celia sent me a text at work. She'd gotten in touch with the real estate company, and they actually had one rental property that had just become available: three bedrooms, one bathroom, and they accepted dogs (which was great because we had two). Unbelievable. All my negative thoughts were totally unfounded.

The lady who owns the real estate company had been out of town on vacation. She just hadn't had time yet to get the rental property posted on her website. Best of all, the price was just $500 per month, easily half the cost of most comparable properties in a place like Asheville. This seemed like it might work out after all.

We went a couple of weekends later to check out the house, and it was great. Plenty of space inside and in a good location: a couple of miles from town, a couple of miles from her parents, and just about a fifteen-minute drive to Danville. The house also sat on sixteen acres, which our dogs would love to explore. There was also a garage and storage building we could use as workshops for projects. (I would later start a woodworking business out of the garage as a side hustle.) It was a great find. We talked specifics with the real estate agent and signed a contract. We'd be able to move in and start our lease on December 15, giving us time over the Christmas break to move all of our stuff.

Assignment one was done. We found a place to live. Now to find an office. This was going to be a challenge.

I knew from the process of searching for a rental house that finding an office would probably be even tougher. I started close to town in Yanceyville, but again there was pretty much nothing online.

I happened to come across a copy of the local newspaper on my future in-laws' kitchen table the weekend we were in town to look at the house and saw an ad for a small office in the same building as the paper. Great! I gave them a call. The room was only $150 per month, but it was very small and had no windows. No thanks. I had to broaden my search to Danville.

Again, Danville is only about fifteen minutes away, and by most standards, that's a short commute compared to bigger cities. I searched online for days. First on Craigslist, then on local real estate websites and even postings in the local paper's classifieds. I didn't find much.

Well, I take that back. I found some places that looked promising but were probably too expensive, especially for my boss Tim. One office in particular had a lot of what I was looking for, but the rent was $550 per month. That meant over the course of a year it would cost almost $7,000, which meant I would have to replicate the good sales year I had in 2015 and *increase* that by at least seven grand to justify the cost. I just shook my head. Then I thought about what we had done to find the rental house. *It was all about word of mouth*.

So I got creative. I called the newly established River District Association, a downtown promotion and tourism organization for Danville, and asked if they knew of any law firms, property owners, or small office holders I could rent from. And it worked! The call ended with them giving me a list of a few names.

The next day I hit the phone and started working through the list. After a lot of phone calls, complete with awkward explanations of my job and what I was looking for, I had narrowed the search to two promising options. The first was a giant empty room across the hall from a dance studio. The other was something akin to what it would look like if a neighborhood handyman tried to build a coworking space without ever visiting one. I coordinated with each property owner and set times to visit during the upcoming Thanksgiving holiday.

The dance studio space was massive. By massive, I mean a 1,000-square-foot room that was designed to serve as storage in this former three-story retail building. The ground level was now an artisan furniture and decor shop. The top level was a dance studio for middle school kids—mostly girls—who were there for several hours every weekday. My office would be a room in the middle that was big enough to fit half a basketball court.

"You think this would be big enough for you?" the building owner joked as he showed me into the space. It was big all right, intimidatingly big. Our voices echoed off the walls as if we were speaking to each other in the bottom of a cave. The room also had these really funky historic windows decorating the back wall.

"I would need you to take out extra insurance for those windows," he made sure to mention as I walked around the room, "and keep in mind those dance classes." "They get in here after lunch and pretty much stay until five."

Not happening.

I couldn't be on the phone all day and have kids dancing and yelling for the whole afternoon. He only wanted $200 per month for rent, but between the pitter patter and chitchat of the dance crew and the additional insurance for windows, this place just wouldn't work. The price couldn't be beat but the situation just wasn't worth it.

Celia and I went later that same day to check out the other place—the home brew coworking space I mentioned earlier. Days before, the owner had emailed me the location and some pictures. We entered the address from the email into Google Maps and made our way there with ease, but as we pulled up to the building we were perplexed. Out front stood a shaggy-haired, middle aged guy with a camera in hand snapping pictures in all directions. He looked out of place, to say the least. Celia and I looked at each other and had the same thought: if this is the guy who owns the building then we might need to keep looking.

"Hi, I'm Barry!" he said with excitement. He extended his arm for a handshake as we stepped out of the car. "You must be Matt."

I confirmed that I was and introduced him to Celia as my fiancée.

"Wow, she's beautiful," he said to me with raised eyebrows and a nudge of the elbow. It was as if we were old college buddies and he hadn't met her yet even though I'd told him all about her. The guy was eccentric, no doubt about it, but there was something instantly comfortable about him.

"Ok, great. Well let me show you inside," he said as he raised his arm toward the front door then reached for his keys.

The building was a former retail shop. It was two stories sandwiched between a makeshift art gallery and one of the oldest men's clothing stores in the city of Danville. Barry had purchased, gutted, and rebuilt almost everything on both the first and second floors. He had created separate office rooms on both levels, each with a door that locked and some that grouped together for larger business operations with multiple employees. Nothing fancy, but serviceable. He had just the right office in mind for me after hearing my description of how recruiting works and how much I'd be on the phone. I could tell he had really given it some thought.

Office number ten sat by itself at the back of the building. It could be easily accessed through the back entrance and wasn't connected to any others, making it quiet enough for all-day phone conversations. Near to the office was the only downstairs bathroom. That was convenient. Just beyond that was the community kitchen area. What more did I need? Best of all, the room had a tall, narrow window with a great view of the Dan River and the newly-constructed, award-winning YMCA on the opposite riverbank.

Perhaps the coolest feature was an old fire door that hung on the back wall. If you've never seen an old industrial fire door just think of a large slab of metal covering an opening in the wall and connected by rope to a weight system. The idea is that if there's a fire the rope will burn, the weight will drop, the door will slide open, and all the building's inhabitants can escape from the flames. Thankfully it was never used.

Barry's price for the office was $295 per month. No window insurance. No long term lease. Nothing funny. I took the contract back to Asheville to discuss with my boss, Tim, and he agreed to make it happen. After adding an internet connection, the total monthly cost for the office would be only about $350 per month. This meant just a little over $4,000 more per year in sales that I'd need to bring in to justify the cost. That was more like it. The lease started January 1, 2016, and I moved all my things in day by day that week.

One of the best perks of the office was its downtown location. Now granted, downtown Danville isn't a bustling metropolis, but it does have a lot of what you might need on a day-to-day basis, or if you're itching for a break from the office. From my location, I could walk to a couple coffee shops if I needed an iced coffee or visit a three-story antique shop with lots of cool old knick-knacks. I could drop into a barber shop for a haircut, go to the bank, and dine at a delicious pizza and sub shop where I would eventually come to eat the same Italian sub combo lunch with my wife just about every Friday. It was a pretty great arrangement.

The quiet of working alone in the back of the building actually made my over-the-phone job a little easier. I could try out new techniques and speak to clients with more confidence knowing if my new approaches didn't work out, no one was close enough to care. Then when I needed a little socialization, someone was almost always milling around Barry's building. 2016 turned out to be my best sales year with the firm and 2017 was even better. The new office had paid off big time for my boss and me.

With both the rental house and office we found, the how-to on accomplishing it was deceptively simple. We just had to look in unorthodox places for what we wanted and then speak directly to people who could help us as quickly as possible.

Sure, the folks I called to inquire about office space probably thought I was crazy. They're a downtown development group after all, but it worked. It worked out well enough for me to bring in sales figures that paid for our wedding, almost entirely covered our honeymoon, and furnished the down payment on our future house (we'll cover those stories in future chapters).

Sure, the online home rental options were abysmal, but the in-person follow-up to the local real estate office did the trick. If you decide to make a similar move to a small town then your best bet may be to simply drive around looking for rental signs, and not spend hours searching the internet.

As I will discuss later, a lot of things for sale or rent in rural areas never even get posted online. But with a little leg work, you can find them.

So here's the lesson for you: when you decide to make your move to a new small town, don't be afraid to call strangers and ask out of the box questions to find what you need. A lot of how business is done in rural America is still done by word of mouth. Use that to your advantage. Before you know it, you may even become the reliable source of information for future newcomers like you.

# Chapter 3
## How To Afford a Pinterest Worthy Wedding

As mentioned earlier, my wife's parents moved to Caswell County a couple of years before we did. They settled into a 1920s farmhouse on ninety acres just outside the town limits of Yanceyville. It's a beautiful property with rolling hills, many wooded acres, a small pond, and gorgeous sunsets stretching southwest into the evening sky. Since getting engaged, Celia and I had often contemplated the setting for our wedding.

The property was unoccupied for about eight years before they bought it, so it needed a bit of a facelift. Nevertheless, we could see the potential. At first, we hesitated to have our wedding there because it was going to require so much work. We looked online at locations all over North Carolina but eventually decided to get married on their farm. After all, the price of the venue—free—couldn't be beat.

And so our work began. Our plan was to have the ceremony in a wooded area about two hundred yards from the main house. Celia picked out a spot in the woods that sloped down toward an old growth oak tree like a natural amphitheater. The reception would be on the other side of the house in what we called "the courtyard." The courtyard was a flat, grassy area set between a nineteenth century cattle barn, a chicken coop, a goat stable, and a new building they had recently built for hay storage for the horses.

Just getting the grounds ready for a wedding was quite a task. For a sense of what it took, allow me to share an incomplete list of the work we did. We killed all the wisteria vines in the backyard, mowed acres and acres of grass, chopped down trees, and created pathways. We built a door to keep the chickens in their coop, spread new gravel over the driveway, planted flowers and shrubs and mulched the front yard flower beds. We're not done yet. We painted the inside of the house, cleaned out truckloads of old clutter, and added support beams to hold up the goat shelter. Then we cleared, cleaned up, and mulched the entire wooded ceremony area. We cleared and burned multiple piles of brush, built benches for seating, built our own directional signs, and did a thousand other decorative things you'd need to do to host about a hundred people for a wedding. The great thing about a lot of this work, though, was that all these projects benefited the property as a whole. So once our wedding was over, we left my in-laws' with a much shorter to-do lists.

As we prepped the property for the wedding, we got to work on all the "official" things we'd need as well. To start, we needed a wedding planner. We searched around and eventually found a group out of Raleigh who offered a great deal on a baseline package. They would help us with the most important details: day-of organizing, setting up tables and chairs, providing vendor contacts, and creating a timeline of when important things needed to happen. This was perfect for us. After all, we were basically building the venue ourselves and had a lot of other people in our lives who could provide the rest.

Talented friends were a fantastic resource. For example, our wedding photographer was one of Celia's friends from a few years before when she worked at an outdoor store. Adam, whose photos for this chapter are posted at www.HowToThinkSmall.com, is an excellent professional photographer. Our videographer was an old college buddy of mine who typically films festivals and concerts, but he had some experience with weddings. We gave him a concept for what we had in mind along with some examples and, no exaggeration, he ended up producing the best wedding video we'd ever seen. For only $750!

For food, we hired two food trucks out of Raleigh, NC—one pizza truck and one taco truck—to provide appetizers and dinner. By food truck price standards, it was expensive, but compared to normal wedding food costs, it was a hell of a deal and way cheaper than a traditional caterer. We also found a local lady, who runs a baking business from her home, to create our wedding cakes. Yes, I said cakes. We wanted multiple, simple cakes instead of one large, elaborate, and over-iced cake that guests normally take two bites of and leave sitting on the table.

The pieces of our wedding were all falling into place, but one area of uncertainty remained: what would we do about an officiant? Like most millennials, Celia and I are not regular church attendees. We didn't want to have an inauthentic religious ceremony that wouldn't be representative of who we are and might be disrespectful to the faith of our guests. After wrestling with the thought for several months, we landed on the perfect person.

Celia had a family friend named Luanne who her mom had met all the way back in 1990 when they first moved to North Carolina. Like Celia's family, Luanne also had four kids, all about the same age as the Spillmanns'. The families were so close that they got together regularly for things like Boy Scouts, camping trips, holiday traditions and more. In fact, it was at an annual tradition of the two families known as "Pie Night" that we asked Luanne to be our officiant. (Pie Night is their annual tradition each Thanksgiving night after dinner when the families get together to indulge in deserts, drinks, and pro football until sometimes after midnight.) At first, Luanne thought we were joking about having her officiate our wedding. But once we convinced her we were serious, she took to the responsibility like a professional.

Luanne was like a second mom to Celia growing up. She was the perfect person for the ceremony and did a fantastic job. Her words moved us, and many in attendance, to laughter and tears. In many states, anyone can be certified online as a wedding officiant, even if they're not religiously ordained. That's how we got Luanne to preside over our wedding and what I'd recommend for anyone in need of an outside-the-box officiant for their special day.

Everything was go for launch. Then a few months before the wedding another problem popped up that called for an immediate decision. It involved the location of our reception. My wife's parents had originally planned to build a new barn for their horses well before our wedding, but the project got delayed because their local contractor was busy with another job. Then about three months before our wedding, the contractor finished the other job and came with an offer to my future in-laws.

He felt confident he could build out the frame of the new barn in time for our wedding. Essentially, he would be constructing a pole barn: a structure with a concrete floor, the primary framing support columns, and a watertight roof with no walls. This was a big decision because we had originally allocated a chunk of the wedding budget to rent a tent for the center of the courtyard I mentioned earlier. With this option, we'd have to shift that money to a new construction project and keep our fingers crossed that it got completed in time. If so, the payoff would be huge. After all, the pole barn—even in its skeleton frame—would be much more weather resistant and roomier than the largest rental tent available.

So contractor Tony and his assistant began work sometime around late February. They measured the footprint of the future barn and dug down to place the plumbing lines and concrete pads. Soon after that, the 12" x 12" posts went up and the roof trusses went on. Before we knew it, the rest of the framing went in and the standing seam panels went on to complete the roof.

With just a few days left until the wedding, the crew poured the concrete that would become the floor. The forecast called for rain that weekend and you don't have to be an engineer to know that concrete can be fickle when setting up and hardening properly. We watched the weather like hawks and to our delight the rain held to a minimum. The temperature ended up being somewhere in the seventies that week. With literally about a day remaining, the concrete dried and we were ready to party. The gamble had paid off! Our new wedding reception venue was complete, and it would prove to be a much nicer setting for the occasion than a rental tent.

Just about everything we did—from creating our own decorations, to building our own seating, to hiring our talented friends, to renting food trucks—saved us a lot of money. Yet we didn't have to compromise on anything. The pictures tell it all; everything turned out absolutely beautiful.

May 27, 2017. Our wedding day had finally arrived and surprisingly I wasn't all that nervous about it. By the time our big day had come, I felt a calm reassurance that I had done all I could to make this occasion as special as it could be. We had physically transformed the property into a one-of-a-kind wedding venue and worked just about every weekend for more than a year to make it happen. I had rehearsed my vows and prepared myself for the emotion of seeing my beautiful bride come down the aisle. Of course, there were more than a few tears. But the best thing about putting in all the work to shape the venue was that the actual wedding felt like the natural conclusion to all the hard work we did.

We had stood in the spot where we'd get married dozens of times. We had walked the property to plot out where all the details would go even more times than that. So when our wedding day came, it was actually nice to take a break from all the work. Knowing we had just accomplished something incredible, we could now enjoy the day with all our family and friends.

Did we get lucky having a huge farm owned by Celia's parents that we could use as our wedding venue? Sure. Anyone without that direct connection would have to pay several thousand dollars for something comparable. However, having a wedding in a similar venue may be as simple as asking for it. If you ride by a farm in your new community with a big, beautiful barn and an open field that might be an excellent venue, stop and knock on the door. My guess is the owners never thought about hosting a wedding there. Maybe you can reserve it for a few hundred bucks. Your rental fee is probably way more than the zero dollars their property brings in most weekends and far less than what an established venue would cost.

Of course, a wedding on a farm may not be for you. That's understandable. So, consider options for other unique, small town venues that would cost you next to nothing. A couple of our local friends, for example, got married at our county's historic courthouse—a pre-Civil War, Italianate work of art designed by architect William Percival—for a rental fee of a mere $100. Local parks and arboretums may also be available, as well as coworking spaces, libraries, breweries, or other historic buildings, all for incredibly affordable costs. Coincidentally, a young couple from Richmond, Virginia, who had originally planned to marry in Apex, North Carolina, ended up using our county's arboretum as their wedding venue when all other locations had been shuttered during the COVID-19 pandemic. Their unique occasion even earned them a write-up in the New York Times.[1]

The bottom line on finding your unique and affordable wedding venue is this: just ask! Be creative. Be respectful. Be prepared for the fact that folks might say no. If the answer is yes, be prepared to put in plenty of hard work. But by all means ask. After all, it just might turn out to be the wedding of your dreams.

---

[1] From "A More Idyllic Setting Was Found," by Nina Reyes, 2020, *The New York Times,* https://www.nytimes.com/2020/05/22/fashion/weddings/a-more-idyllic-setting-was-found.html

# Chapter 4
## How To Get Involved and Make a Difference

Maybe it's because I'm somewhat of a political nerd, but almost as soon as we moved to Caswell County I attended my first county commission meeting. I can't remember what was on the agenda or what night of the week it was, but one thing stood out that I'll never forget: the noticeable lack of citizens in attendance.

It felt like the stereotypical scene from an old Western movie. The newcomer enters the saloon. The regulars and the bartender pause for a second to check him out and make sure he's not a threat then go back about their business. I was the new guy walking into the saloon for the first time. Coming from my experience with the activist crowd in Asheville, I was used to standing-room-only public meetings with citizens cheering, hissing, and eagerly signing the roster for their three minutes at the microphone. At this commission meeting, however, aside from the elected officials, I was one of only maybe four or five people in attendance.

I returned home that night and thought surely this was a fluke; there's no way most of their meetings were like this. So I went online to the local newspaper's website, and it was a similar scene. There were hardly any recent stories covering local politics at all. In fact, they had more stories about an old cat that slinked around their office than they did about local elected officials. It took quite a bit of doing my own research just to find the names of all the politicians in the county.

Despite the relative dullness, I continued to attend local public meetings and stay engaged. At the county school board meeting, I was one of two guests in the room. Heck, at a board of elections meeting, it was just the board and me. Though there wasn't a whole lot of action at these meetings, it did give me great insight into what was happening in the community. Almost always, I could ask questions during meetings if I had them. I could also stay after and ask board members about the current issues on the agenda, past issues, and what they thought might be coming up in the near future. It gave me a pretty full picture of the local issues in a relatively short period of time.

More importantly, this involvement helped me to directly connect with people of importance in the community. At county commission meetings, I got to know each of our commissioners. I was quickly on a first name basis with the county manager, county attorney, and clerk to the board. At the board of elections meeting, I got to know the head of our county's VFW; one of the most respected Vietnam veterans in our area.

Getting to know these folks almost immediately opened opportunities for me. The county clerk served on the county's historical association board along with the wife of the VFW leader. Not too long after meeting them, and expressing some interest, I was asked to join the Caswell County Historical Association and became a board member. This was just a few months after moving to the county. A few months later I applied to serve on the county's newly formed "Heritage and Cultural Preservation Committee." This was a board created to make recommendations on public art and historic monuments donated to the county. Since I was now a member of the historical association board, I had a little more credibility to qualify for the position. The commissioners appointed me at the next meeting after I applied.

It was around that time I found out that I lived in the same neighborhood as one of our county commissioners. He also served as the administrator for the small, non-profit water system serving the seventy-five or so houses in our vicinity. The West Yanceyville Water System Board did things such as ensure the water sources were clean, set water rates for customers, and allocate money for any needed repairs. Around the same time that I found out the commissioner was my neighbor, another board member chose to retire from the water system board. So my commissioner neighbor asked if I'd like to join the board, and I accepted. Before I knew it, I was serving on three local boards, all with different responsibilities and diverse connections—all within a year of moving to the community.

Soon after, another county commissioner asked me to join a non-profit he had just formed to benefit low income youth. I did. Not long after that, our county manager asked me to serve on an advisory board for the community college's new Emergency Services Advisory Council. The council was assembled to give the community college some guidance on what they should teach new paramedic students. At first I thought, "I have no business being on this committee. I have no emergency service experience whatsoever." Thankfully, that didn't matter to them. In fact, they actively sought two panel members who were just regular citizens in order to gain a wider range of input. Plus, the board only met twice a year, so it was entirely doable to fit it into my schedule.

At this point, I was serving on so many boards and commissions that I had to actively deny requests to join new ones.

Aside from the fact that all this volunteerism helped to pad my resume, the greatest benefit of all this service was that I actually got to help my community in a meaningful way. My involvement with the Historical Association led to us hosting the largest heritage festival in the organization's history. The festival was organized around honoring our county's World War I veterans on the 100th anniversary of the war. Descendants of local veterans came from tens if not hundreds of miles away to see their ancestors honored publicly. We even had one of our US senators fly an American flag over the Capitol building for a day in their honor.

My involvement with the youth nonprofit EPIC Caswell (Empowering Personal Initiative and Creativity) allowed me to help with multiple hiking and kayaking trips around the region. Most of these kids came from very low-income households. Some had never even traveled beyond the county line. It was an incredible feeling to take them on a road trip to their first big city, on their first hike up a mountain, and for their first time paddling out on a kayak.

My involvement with the Heritage and Cultural Preservation Committee allowed me to help shape a small sliver of county ordinance policy. That experience really paid off when I was hired as the county planner, but I will cover that later.

My time on the water system board provided me with a look into how public utilities are managed. It also offered insight into when it is appropriate to forgive someone's late water bill because they had trouble paying it, for example, or because their pipe burst in the middle of winter. Every experience was different, but they all mattered.

Almost all of this involvement stemmed from attending a few public meetings when hardly anyone else did. I am not particularly gifted in any of the areas I mentioned above, I was just willing to show up and pitch in.

Small towns and rural counties all across America are in the same boat. The vast majority of their meetings are poorly attended. Citizens usually don't pay attention to what's on a local board's agenda until it directly affects them. *And there's nothing wrong with that!* People lead busy lives, and public meetings are usually very boring. (I have since been part of *several* standing-room-only local meetings that were quite the opposite, trust me!). However, that can be an advantage for someone looking to make a difference. Be the person willing to show up and get to know what's going on when no one else seems to care. It pays off!

Obviously most of my volunteering involved historical boards or policy making. But don't assume that is the only path. Apply the same approach to your passions. Everywhere you look in rural America, a parks and recreation league is desperate for energetic adults to coach or organize sporting events. The same is true for nonprofits organizing food drives or churches collecting coats for the needy. Do you know how overjoyed a small-town charity would be to have someone like you just run their Facebook page? You would instantly be their hero.

This type of involvement will help boost your credibility and pad your resume. (It even helped me get my current job—see Chapter 6). But most importantly, it soothes your soul. Just keep in mind that you must approach your community engagement with a pure heart. You should genuinely want to make a positive change in your community before you attend your first meeting or fill out your first board application. If not, those currently in a position of power will sense it. You will not earn their trust. But genuine interest and commitment can very quickly lead to having meaningful impacts on your new community.

So how can you get involved and make a difference after making your move to rural America? It's easy. Attend local meetings. Find out what local boards, committees, or nonprofits might need your help. Be willing to do the tasks others don't want to do or can't. Ask questions and get to know the people already in a position of power. Say yes to what feels right. Don't be afraid to say no if you don't have the time or don't think it's a fit. Always follow through with what you say you'll do. Begin the work with true intentions to make a meaningful difference. In no time at all, you and your community will both be better off for it...even if it's something as simple as a kid's first hiking trip.

# Chapter 5
## How To Buy a House for $39,000

Even before Celia and I got married, we started looking around the area for a house. Caswell County is filled with some beautiful historic homes and those are the ones we set our sights on to plant our lives and grow our future family. But the pickin's were slim, as they say, and just like before when trying to find rental properties, online listings were limited. However, we came to the mutual agreement that we were willing to put in the work to fix up a house if needed so we didn't necessarily need something that was move-in ready. In fact, our goal quickly became finding a fixer-upper that would give us the dual accomplishment of a finished house with historic charm but modern features. And after some searching, we found exactly what we were looking for.

Our search started online, of course, and Zillow was generally the most helpful site. The same real estate agency we used to find our rental house had some online postings as well. However, much of what we found just wasn't the right fit. The houses we found were either too small or would have required way too much work. For example, we found homes with a good number of bed-rooms and bathrooms, but the kitchen was way too small, which meant we'd have to remove several walls or really crack open the house to achieve the layout we wanted. Since the total number of homes online was limited, we quickly ran through those options and crossed them off our list. It was time to get out and find one ourselves.

It actually didn't take us that long to find homes with for sale signs out front. Like a lot of items in rural areas, we've discovered that houses, cars, trucks, farm equipment, and other things sell by word of mouth and person-to-person. One day in the mid-winter of 2017, I was riding through Yanceyville and noticed a new for sale sign in front of a house I had ridden by once or twice before. The sign had only a phone number on it. No list-ing of bedrooms, bathrooms, or even a price. It was a Craftsman style house on the same block as some other nice historic homes. It didn't look like anything particu-larly special but it looked nice enough. I decided to call the number on the sign just to give it a shot and set up an appointment to view it.

The owner was a guy named Roger who actually lived in Greensboro, a larger city about forty-five minutes away. For one reason or another, he had been quite active with various things in Caswell County over the years. Not only did he own this home and a few others in the county, he was also a former board member of the Historical Association that I talked about in the last chapter. The fact that I was on the board now gave us an instant connection and I think helped him trust that I was a serious potential buyer. We made arrangements to tour the house on a Saturday in March; it was actually the same weekend Celia was away in New Orleans for her bachelorette party, so I had to go it alone.

We met out front at the arranged time, introduced ourselves, and began our tour. As soon as he opened the door, I was blown away. Not because the house was particularly nice, but because it was huge. You couldn't tell from the road but this house was just under three thousand square feet. Technically, it was five bedrooms with two and a half baths, though two of the "bedrooms" were used for other purposes. The house was built in 1929 and featured the original hardwood floors, decorative door and window moldings, foundation, framing, fireplaces, and built in cabinets.

A renovation had been done to the house in 1994, which added a master bathroom, mudroom, second full bathroom, and laundry room. All of those rooms were nice and spacious, despite being comically outdated. In fact, most of the house was comically outdated. The kitchen featured a ceiling fan (for some reason) and linoleum floors that covered the original hardwoods. The living room featured crown molding that didn't even touch the ceiling and a shimmery purple wallpaper on every wall. But the master bathroom was my favorite. Almost the entire room was covered in powder blue and pink tiles; as if decorated by a loving grandmother in the mid-1980's who didn't know whether to expect a new boy or girl grandchild from the hospital so she tried to compromise with both. There was also a nice, big backyard and a three hundred square foot workshop out back. Behind the property was nothing but untouched woods and the home next door was a beautiful old cottage that had been built before the Civil War.

The house definitely needed some work, but I could easily see the potential. I snapped pictures on my phone in every room as we went along to send them all to Celia in New Orleans. Unlike the other houses we looked at, this one wouldn't force us to compromise with small bathrooms or tearing open too many walls. I told Roger I was definitely interested but I'd have to talk to my fiancée about it once she was back in town before we could make a final decision. He understood.

Before we parted ways he told me his list price. "I'm asking $39,900," he said, "and not a penny less."

I had to stop myself from outwardly reacting to what was going through my mind. In fact, it took me a moment to process what he just said.

"Holy hell!" I thought. "This guy only wants $40,000 for this house?!" With his eyes squinting slightly back at me, he must have read my slightly numb reaction and thought it awkward.

I finally blurted something like, "Sounds great!" "That seems like that's like…a good price," or some such nonsense. I sent texts to Celia with all the pictures and the asking price. She and her friends at the bachelorette party couldn't believe it, especially for that cheap. One of them was from Las Vegas, and said with amazement: "Thirty-nine thousand? That's less than what I paid for my down payment!"

Not long after Celia returned from New Orleans, we toured the house together. She was as enamored with it as I was. We made the decision to go for it after the wedding, though we knew it would be a big project. As we sat in the Miami airport on our way to honeymoon in Costa Rica, I called Roger and told him we'd like to move forward. He assured us that he would not sell the house while we were out of the country since we were the most serious buyers yet to show interest. This gave us a little extra peace of mind during our honeymoon, but we knew we were in for quite the process once we got back.

Almost as soon as we returned from Central America it was show time. I called Roger to let him know we were going to start working with the bank and a contractor about securing financing and developing plans for the remodel. Though things began happening quickly for us, there was absolutely no way we could have taken this much time with a home purchase in a larger city. At the time, my best friend was living in Nashville, Tennessee, and he used to tell me wild stories about how homes in his neighborhood would have buyers lined up with cash deposits ready even before they technically hit the market. Other older homes there would be demolished and have the land graded for a new foundation the same day.

Roger was friendly about the whole thing and even gave us some advice on local contractors to call. Part of our challenge was that we'd have to get a contractor from the next county over. Tony, the only local guy we knew who could do the job, was now busy finishing up the barn for my in-laws. Plus, we couldn't exactly pull one from Danville since licensing requirements don't cross state lines.

Another problem was, believe it or not, the home price was too low for us to finance it through the bank. Forty thousand dollars was way too much for us to pay out of pocket, but through this process we learned that banks don't like to finance homes under $50,000 in total value. So we had to get creative. Luckily, we found a bank in town that did home purchase and construction loans as a bundle. Best of all, they would only require ten percent down to finance the loan.

Around that same time, we found a contractor from a town about thirty minutes away that looked up to the task. Their business model involved new construction, remodels, and disaster repair. Perfect! We scheduled their estimator to look house over and give us some figures on what it would cost to do the major work that we couldn't do on our own. He looked the house up and down and talked with us about the renovations we had in mind.

At the conclusion of his inspection, we also let him know Roger's asking price. He raised his eyebrows and responded with a smirk, saying, "If y'all don't buy this house then let me know, cuz I might."

We took that as a good sign.

A week or two later, the contractor got back to us with an estimate. Structurally, the house was in excellent shape. Our plan was to have the contractor totally remodel the master bathroom, remove a wall to double the size of the master bedroom, replace virtually everything in the kitchen, rebuild the front porch, and upgrade load bearing walls, electrical wiring, and plumbing throughout the house. Their cost estimate was $75,000. We would handle everything else, mostly cosmetic projects.

I took the report and itemized estimate back to Roger and told him I'd like for us to draft a purchase agreement. Given that we would have to repair some foundation and utility-related issues I asked him for a reduction in the price. I offered $39,000 even. That was $900 off his original price but two and a quarter percent of the total price. That same percentage off the average home price in America would be more than $5,000. After some hesitation, he took the deal.

Now we had some real numbers to take to the bank. Remember, they wouldn't finance anything under $50,000, but when we added the $39,000 home price to the $75,000 construction budget, it gave us a total loan estimate of $114,000. This was certainly much more feasible for the bank and, in fact, still much lower than the home prices they were used to financing, especially out of their Raleigh branch.

I won't lie, the paperwork was still a nightmare. Between the bank, the lawyers, and the contractors—and all of them seeming to take as many days off as possible for every passing holiday—the closing process took us a few months. But on Halloween Day, 2017, the wait was finally over. We went to the lawyer's office that afternoon with a certified check for ten percent down and the expectation that we'd have to sign a mountain of paperwork. It's a good thing we were prepared. We left the office over an hour later with the keys to our brand new, $39,000 house. It was time to call the contractors in and roll up our sleeves. Move-in day was going to be as soon as we could make it.

A word of caution here. Like me, you've probably seen plenty of HGTV shows where a young couple buys a house and then all of their friends and family rush in wearing matching T-shirts to gleefully help them fix it up. That won't happen. Unless you're luckier than me, virtually no one will help you renovate your house. They will be happy for you and wish you all the best, but most of them won't do so much as lift a paint brush. Only a few saintly friends and family members proved to be the exception to this rule.

If you're going to try a renovation job yourself, here's my advice. One, do as much work as you can before you move in. This makes making a mess and having space to work much easier. Two, start in a low traffic area of the house. No one will notice the badly patched drywall or offset crown molding in your utility room. But odds are they will notice it in your front entrance. Three, ask for assistance with the big stuff. As mentioned above, no one will be working on this thing like you will. However, if a remodel task involves a heavy lift or painting an outdoor space before a rainstorm hits then don't be afraid to ask for help. If you give specific instructions and a specific task you need help with then your reluctant friends and family will be more apt to lend a hand.

Side note: there are few things in this world that most dudes love more than demolition. If your project involves fully gutting a bathroom or kitchen, invite over the most testosterone loaded friend you have, give him a sledgehammer and a buy him a case of beer. Before you know it, those old cabinets will be a pile of splinters on their way to the dump.

Our contractors got to work just after Thanksgiving that year and started with the master bath. I gave them an assist by fully gutting the room on free weekends in November. Once they finished the master bedroom and bathroom, they rebuilt the front porch then got to work on the kitchen. A friend and I also fully gutted the kitchen prior to them working there. As a result of this demolition work, we saved $3,000 in labor off the contractor's total price tag.

It was in the course of gutting the kitchen that we found the original hardwood floors under the linoleum.

Refinishing these floors instead of laying all new tile saved us an additional few thousand bucks there as well. We were then able to use that money to buy a brand new, tankless water heater. It's been an unexpected luxury. By the time the contractors finished their work, we were able to save or reallocate thousands of dollars within their budget just by doing a little advance work and taking advantage of creative opportunities. That eventually meant less money the bank paid them and, as a result, a lower monthly mortgage payment for us.

The contractors finished the first phase a few months after they started. In March of 2018, we moved in before they renovated the kitchen. It was a challenge to live with a temporary kitchen for a while, but we made it through. As the contractors concluded their work, we picked up where they left off. Almost every room in the house required something: the removal of the old wallpaper, scraping down popcorn ceilings, patching cracks and holes in walls, new paint, new trim, new tile—even the full remodel of two spare bathrooms. It was a lot of work, but we got it done. Personally, it's the biggest project I've ever completed in my life, and it felt incredibly rewarding to have it done. The house isn't perfect, but it's perfect for us, and way more affordable than what we'd spend for a house almost anywhere else.

Now I'm sure you're asking yourself: "How the hell does anyone find a house for $39,000, even in a small town that's not a total mess and falling in on itself?" So let me tell you how we came to find our house for that price. First off, home prices in general in our area are low. Not a lot of folks are rushing into Yanceyville, which puts downward pressure on home values.

A local family had lived in our house until 2007 when they fell victim to the Great Recession and could no longer afford to live there. They sold the house, to Roger, for cheap. Forty-five thousand dollars, I believe. At the same time, Roger purchased the pre-Civil War era cottage next door and started in on fixing that one up first. That project took him a few years, and once it was complete, he didn't have the appetite to remodel ours as well, though he had originally planned it. So, for years and years, the house just sat there unoccupied. During that time, Roger put on a brand new roof, installed all new windows, weatherized all the utilities, and maintained the grounds. Eventually, he got tired of trying to rent and/or sell it and just kept lowering the price until he got a serious buyer. That's when we came in.

Our circumstance was rare, but it happened for us. It can happen for you too. A lot of small and mid-sized cities out there experienced an economic boom decades ago and since then their populations have fled to somewhere else. There are also plenty of beautiful homes in rural areas where families left long ago for life in a bigger city. In fact, according to the National Association of Realtors' County Median Home Prices and Monthly Mortgage Payment statistical map[2], sixty percent of all US counties feature an average home price of less than $150,000. Coincidentally, of course, they happen to be many of the most rural counties in the country.

This means there's a great deal of real estate in these areas at bargain prices that can be transformed into your dream home. They're just sitting there waiting for a new life. You just have to be willing to look carefully and put in the work to find them. You'll also need some elbow grease, a good contractor, and the help of a bank. But

---

[2] National Association of Realtors. (2020, June 7). *Research and Statistics: County Median Home Prices and Monthly Mortgage Payment.* https://www.nar.realtor/research-and-statistics/housing-statistics/county-median-home-prices-and-monthly-mortgage-payment.

with that and the right mindset you just might find your own dream house for a mere $39,000.

# Chapter 6
## How to Land a County Planner Job with No Experience

To say I had *no* experience isn't exactly true. But there's no way I would have been hired as our county's planning director if I had to compete with more experienced applicants in a larger metro area. Landing this job was the confluence of being in the right place at the right time, with the right conditions, and just enough qualifications to make me a decent candidate for the job. Here's how it happened.

As I detailed in Chapter 4, Celia and I got involved with local boards, commissions, and nonprofits almost immediately after moving to Caswell County. This experience not only allowed us to serve our community in a genuine way, but it helped us to make some incredibly valuable connections as well.

One of those contacts was with our county manager. He and I had become close acquaintances in the months since we first met at those lonely commissioners' meetings from Chapter 4. He even nominated me to serve on that EMS advisory council. In the late spring of

2018, I happened to run into him one day outside of our town's historic courthouse. By then, I had managed to switch my remote office location to an empty room upstairs in the county's historical museum. The museum was actually walking distance from our new house and the rent was cheaper than my old Danville office. It was another win-win for both me and my boss.

"Hi Matthew, how are things going with you?" Bryan asked me.

"Not great, actually," I responded.

I proceeded to express to him some frustrations with my current job. Despite the nice new office, I had clients paying me late and candidates not showing up for job interviews. On a couple of occasions, I even had *clients* not showing up for interviews. The recruiting job I had held for the past several years had run its course. It was time to move on.

"Well you heard our county planner position is opening up, didn't you?" he inquired.

"I had no idea," I told him. Honestly, I wasn't even one hundred percent sure what the county planner did.

"Yep, our current planner has decided she's going to Chapel Hill in the fall to get her master's degree. We just started taking applications," he informed me. "I certainly can't guarantee you'll get the job, but you should apply if you're interested."

The county manager and I talked a little longer that day about the job and the application process. As he explained things to me, they made a lot more sense. The county planner is the person in local government who authorizes all new subdivision plans, deals with zoning issues, reviews development proposals, and, in general, has to understand how state and local laws govern new construction and development throughout the county.

"Perfect!" I thought. In a roundabout way these were all things I had learned through my current job.

In the recruiting world, especially construction recruiting, I focused a lot on ensuring that the candidate for each job had skills specific to their trade. Whether it was residential, commercial, or any other type of construction, it was my job to know just enough about each to ensure that the candidate would be a good fit for the position. This often included knowing how land development, zoning compliance, and permitting played a role in their processes. Beyond that, one of the coolest things about working at that particular firm was that the owner was an elected House member in the North Carolina General Assembly. In fact, he was voted the most effective legislator in the state a year or two earlier. So talking with him regularly about the bills being passed in Raleigh and the general nature of regulations and the law gave me great insight into the effects of state and local code. Basically, when it came to understanding the regulatory landscape of local government, a big component of the job, I had more of a head start than I realized.

I revised my resume, drafted a cover letter, and applied for the job a few days later. In the meantime, I'll admit I was in a bit of a panic. After all, I didn't go to school to become a planner, and I had never even worked in a planning and zoning department, let alone any job in local government. So I did absolutely as much online research as possible. Luckily, I found out that the current Yanceyville town manager used to work as our county planner, and so I scheduled a meeting with him to ask as much as I could about the job. I also contacted an intern with the Danville Regional Foundation through my wife's job—more about that later—who had just graduated college with a degree in urban planning. When I got him on the phone, I asked as many questions as possible about the official nature of planning from an academic perspective. I even called our county's economic development director to get perspective on how her and the county planner worked together on various projects.

After as much preparation as I could handle, I felt about as prepared as I was going to be. The interview lasted close to an hour; it was me, the county manager, and the county's human resources director. I left the interview thinking it went pretty well. And it turned out I was right.

A couple of weeks later, I was called back for a second interview. This time I met with the chief building inspector and environmental health director in the county manager's office. Those departments share an office with the county planning department. We talked for maybe thirty minutes about the expectations of the job, the office culture, and some of the things they'd like to see done differently now that a new planner was stepping in. At the conclusion of that meeting, Bryan offered me the job. I told him I'd take it. I was overjoyed. This was not only going to be a very positive step for my career, but it was going to allow me to positively impact my community in a full-time capacity. It was a perfect fit at the perfect time.

I then had a pretty tough phone call to make to my old boss back in Asheville. I had worked for him for just about seven years at that point, and I feared that he would be fairly upset. I swallowed hard and made the call. I was nervous.

To my surprise, he understood my reasons for wanting to make the change and that it would give me the opportunity to directly contribute to the growth of our new community. He even offered to let me stay connected to the firm and be able to make some money on the side.

"I'll hate to see you go," he told me, "but maybe you could stay on in a part-time capacity?"

It was an intriguing offer. After all, many of my clients were on the West Coast. That meant I'd have three hours after work every day when they'd still be open for business. I thought about it for a bit but ultimately had to turn that down. I knew it would be too much to obligate myself to at least eleven hours of work per day.

"What if I stayed on in a commission-only basis?" I countered. No regular salary, just the bonus money that would come in if I closed a deal.

He paused for a moment then agreed to the arrangement. This meant I'd be able to set up my work phone and computer at home and have the opportunity to close deals from time to time, on my own schedule. In other words, I'd have a new full-time job with excellent benefits *and* be able to bring in some extra cash on the side. How lucky could I be? Things were working out perfectly.

The community investment of time and energy that Celia and I had made when we first moved to the county had just paid off in a big way.

My first official day as county planner started in the summer of 2018. I was overjoyed to take the job, and I still love it to this day. After a few months learning the fundamentals, and making sure I wasn't screwing anything up, I was even given the freedom to launch my own initiative.

Caswell remains one of the most technology starved counties in the entire state of North Carolina. That's true whether it comes to cell phone service or broadband internet. Coincidentally, one of the roles of the county planner is to review applications for any new cell towers to be built in the county, which often relates closely to internet connectivity issues as well. Meanwhile, the North Carolina General Assembly had added a grant program into the budget that year that would reward up to $10 million for rural broadband expansion. I discussed this grant program and some ideas of my own with Bryan, and he gave me the green light to start my own project. In December of 2018, I launched an initiative called Connect Caswell 2020.

The initiative was aimed at paving the way for every citizen in our county who wanted it to have access to high-speed internet and reliable cell service. I'm proud to say that with some creative community outreach, some incredibly hard work from several local residents, and a great partnership with a broadband provider out of Charlotte we were successful. In May of 2019, North Carolina's governor announced that roughly $1.5 million of the total $10 million allocated would go toward broadband internet expansion in Caswell County. To this day, it remains the greatest accomplishment of my professional life.

Furthermore, as of this writing, the county is entrusting me to formulate plans that would implement county-wide zoning for the first time in our history. This is an incredible responsibility—and honor—that I've been given. It's hard to fathom that someone who isn't from this area would have earned enough trust from those in charge for such a task, but that's where I sit. And I know without a doubt I wouldn't be in a similar situation in a larger city.

On a side note, allow me to tell a similar story of how Celia landed a great local job even before I got mine.

Beyond all the local boards and commissions that I had joined, my wife, Celia, got involved with many of her own. Our involvement put us in regular contact with several of our county commissioners, with whom we developed a great rapport. At one local event, a commissioner pulled Celia aside and encouraged her to apply for an internship with a nonprofit called the Danville Regional Foundation. DRF, as many locals call it, is one of the largest grant-making organizations in the area. They focus on education, economic development, health, and wellness within the region.

Celia applied a short time later under the assumption that a summer internship with them would be a great foot in the door to a job in the area once the internship was over. Her application got her an initial phone interview with DRF but then, to her dismay, she never heard anything back. After a while, she was a bit disheartened that they seemed not even to want her as an intern, despite having a master's degree.

As soon as she assumed her shot had passed, she swallowed her pride and sent them an email to thank them for the interview. To her surprise, they responded almost immediately.

"Celia, we don't want you to be an intern," their senior program officer told her. "We want you to apply to be a fellow with DRF."

A fellowship with them was much more than a simple internship. Fellows were full-time employees for at least two years. Fellows could craft their own initiatives and had their own line of project funding. Not to mention the salary and benefits that would come with the full-time position. It was a fantastic opportunity.

She went in for that interview a few days later and got the job. Celia served as a fellow with DRF for two years and during that time she pioneered a study into our region's entrepreneur ecosystem. Basically, the work she did informed our entire region's knowledge of the gig

economy and how residents—younger people especially—were using internet connectivity and apps like
Uber and Etsy to set their own work parameters or sell
their own products. This was quite innovative work for a
region with generations of families who had worked on
tobacco farms and in textile mills. Once her fellowship
ended, a nearby Danville-based business incubator used
the research to create a new full-time position under their
umbrella to continue the work for the region in perpetu-
ity.

Celia, on the other hand, started her own new ven-
ture after her time with DRF ended. She became the
owner and operator of Caswell Flower Company, a sustainable flower farm that operates on the same land
where we got married a few years ago. She's already become known as "the flower lady" around town and is
without a doubt the best-known flower farmer in our region. In fact, at the time of this writing, she already has
several weddings booked for the remainder of the year,
though many have been postponed or altered due to
COVID-19 precautions.

All of these job and career opportunities have
taught us one thing: there's a great chance that none of

this would have been available to us in a big city. To replicate this success in larger markets you often need some combination of years of experience, the right connections, and an advanced college degree. Of course, family ties or wealthy friends wouldn't hurt. But even with that, you'll probably spend several years under the management of some baby boomer boss who should have retired years ago before you can get to where you want.

The other lesson is to constantly keep your eyes open for new opportunities. Whether it was my job, Celia's fellowship, or starting the flower business, the common theme is that we seized on an opportunity when the moment was right. In the case of the flower business, she took advantage of the fact that the market for the product was virtually wide open. And sure, job openings like mine come up in larger cities too, but the difference there is you may be one of maybe dozens or even hundreds of applicants. When I interviewed for the planning job, I think I was one of only five or six.

So whatever your passion is, or wherever you want your career to go, stay vigilant about seizing opportunities when you make your move to rural America. Even if you bring limited experience to the job, there's a good chance you'll be in the mix with a small pool of applicants with similar credentials. Even if you don't feel as though you have enough experience to apply, you just might surprise yourself and land the most rewarding and meaningful job of your career.

# Chapter 7
## How To Build a Meaningful Life
## in Rural America

I'd like to begin this final chapter by offering a glimpse into what my day-to-day life is like now. Then I'll provide data that leads me to believe your life would be better outside of a big city as well. Finally, I'll finish with a brief how-to guide for building your future in rural America.

Most days I wake up about thirty minutes before I have to be at work. I leave the house with about ten minutes to spare. That's because it takes me about five minutes to walk to my office. That's right—walk. On days when I ride my bike, it takes me only about a minute and a half to get there.

When I need to get a haircut, I walk there too. The post office is next door to my office. Our county library, parks and recreation facility, a bike shop, a hardware store, a fitness center, the town municipal building, the county courthouse, our voting precinct site, and a few convenience stores are all within walking distance of our house as well. And it's all connected by a pretty nice municipal sidewalk system. It is unbelievably convenient. Several of our local friends jokingly refer to me as "Yanceyville's only bike commuter." If we really needed to walk to the nearest grocery store, we could, but it's also no more than a bike ride away. Of course, what we don't get there we're able to buy from quite a few friends who grow organic produce on their farms. Our yard size and zoning allowances also make it possible to have a few things to pick from in our own vegetable and herb garden.

When I leave work for the day I'm usually home by 5:10 p.m. at the latest. On days when I take just a half hour for lunch and leave early, I'm home before five. I feel terrible for folks in larger metro areas who are stuck in a car for sometimes several hours a day just to get to and from work. When my daughter is older, this will make a huge difference when I need to shuttle her to and from sporting events or after-hours school functions.

Without a doubt, one of the best perks about the location of our house is the walkability of our neighborhood. We live right on the outskirts of what you might classify as "downtown." If you leave our house and head away from the town center our road quickly becomes a beautiful country parkway with rolling hills and long-range views. About a mile from our house is the town's water intake and treatment facility. We often walk the route to the water plant for an evening stroll before or after dinner and usually don't even get passed by a car. In fact, even though we're still inside town limits, we are often able to walk there and back with nothing but the sound of nature around us. Not a car drives by, not a plane flies overhead, no man-made sounds echo through the trees.

Though we live in a small town, we also have weekly curbside trash pickup, public water and sewer, and excellent internet service. And if we ever do have issues with town services, we often get a call back directly from the mayor or the town manager, who has become a good friend of ours. I can guarantee this isn't the type of accommodation you'll find in bigger cities.

And of course, I'd be remiss if I didn't mention how the COVID-19 outbreak affected—or in essence didn't really affect—our lives during the stay-at-home orders of spring 2020. Though we did stay in as much as possible—especially after our baby was born—my wife continued her five-minute commute to work on her flower farm, and I was still able to walk to work on days when I needed to go in. Mostly, I just worked from home.

Our walks down to the water treatment facility continued, as did exercise at the tennis courts less than a mile from our house, and a mountain bike outing with some friends on the trails about two miles away. In other words, not only did our lives not change much during the pandemic, we actually had a little more time and space to enjoy the amenities so close to home. Though our daughter was born in the midst of a global shutdown, we had no problem strolling her around the vacant sidewalks of Yanceyville to coax her into a nap on a daily basis. We have achieved the work-life balance that our peers seek in major cities but at less than half the cost. Our location, neighborhood, and lifestyle allow us to save money on gas, have more free time in the evenings, get outdoors more often, and spend money more consciously.

A lot of people ask us about the downsides of living in a small town, such as having to drive an hour or so to major cities or a lack of restaurant options. But what we've realized is that the trade-off is so much better. For example, it's allowed me to pay off all of my student loan debt. I don't know many other millennial's who have done that.

By having a lower cost of living, and not dining out like we used to, it actually affords us much more of an opportunity to do things like take big trips more often. In 2018, for example, we drove to Utah where Celia ran a half marathon in Zion National Park. In the fall of 2019, we made a road trip to Bozeman, Montana for Celia to attend a multi-day floral design workshop. It was our first trip back to Montana since we got engaged there. We had an absolute blast and made several new friends from all over the country.

There's no way we could have afforded to do these things if we had the day-to-day overhead costs of living in a bigger city.

Speaking of Montana, a rural sliver of the state was recently featured PBS *NewsHour* segment[3] that helped inspire me to write this book. According to that December 2, 2019 report, and the *Wall Street Journal* article[4] it cited,

---

[3] From "Why Millennials are Moving Away from Large Urban Centers," 2019, PBS *NewsHour*,
https://www.youtube.com/watch?v=mjZu5AU3NYI.
[4] From "Millennials Continue to Leave Big Cities," by J. Adamy and P. Overberg, 2019, *The Wall Street Journal*,

U.S. cities with a population above 500,000 collectively lost about 30,000 millennials and young Gen X'ers in 2018. "It was the fourth consecutive year that big cities saw this population of young adults shrink," the *Wall Street Journal* article states. And as the dust settles on COVID-19 I believe this trend will continue. According to the April 2, 2020 Redfin article entitled, "Interest in Rural Areas and Small Town Spikes During the Coronavirus Outbreak",[5] "As of March 23, the seven-day average year-over-year change in pageviews of homes in rural areas and small towns were up 115% and 88% respectively. Pageviews for homes in urban metro areas with populations of 1 million or more decreased 10% over the same period."

That same PBS *NewsHour* story partially profiles a young professional entrepreneur named Katherine Rose and her business KRose Marketing. As Katherine put it, "I was actually the first company to sell cattle on social media that we know of." The KRose website, www.KRose-Marketing.com, further explains that Katherine's

https://www.wsj.com/articles/millennials-continue-to-leave-big-cities-11569470460, 2019 by Dow Jones & Company, Inc.

[5] From "Interest in Rural Areas and Small Towns Spikes During the Coronavirus Outbreak," by T. Ellis, 2020, *Redfin*, https://www.redfin.com/blog/urban-vs-rural-homebuyer-interest-coronavirus

company started out with a sole focus on agriculture but has since evolved to include digital marketing training and education. Katherine's is the new story of entrepreneurship in rural America and reminds me a lot of my wife's company.

Caswell Flower Company actually started as a handmade paper business that featured flower seeds embedded into the fibers. Thus, when someone receives a thank you or birthday card on Celia's paper, they're able to plant it in soil, water it, and watch the wildflowers grow. Then one day Celia thought, "why don't I just grow the flowers myself?" and off she went. Now her arranged flowers for weddings, special events, farmers markets, and more, are the centerpiece of her business.

Like Katherine, and undoubtedly countless others, Celia started her business with one model in mind then adapted it to fit the local need. At the core of these small business innovations are the recognition of a void in the local market, a willingness to experiment, the security of knowing that risks in rural areas are less costly, and marketing skills adapted from what they learned in college or a bigger city. These are techniques you can take advantage of as well, except, in rural America you'll actually get noticed and appreciated for them. In a large metro you would usually just get drowned out in the noise.

Zooming out even more, take a look at the larger trend that Celia's business is a part of. Today more than ever, younger, college-educated women are making their careers in agriculture. An April 12, 2019 *Pacific Standard* magazine article, "Agriculture Census Data Shows The U.S. Has More Female Farmers Than Ever", [6] states: "Over the last five years, the number of male farmers fell, while the number of women rose: Female producers now make up 36 percent of farmers, a 27 percent increase from 2012." The article goes on to cite: "Now, 56 percent of farms have at least one female producer," even if the head of the farm is male. Obviously, trends in agriculture reflect just one sector of rural economies. However, this trend speaks to two things important for your consideration: first, the innovations taking place in rural communities are opening doors to more diverse groups of people and, second, taking advantage of such trends allows you to bring autonomy and meaning back into your work.

---

[6] From "Agriculture Census Data Shows the U.S. has More Female Farmers than Ever," by E. Moon, 2019, *Pacific Standard*, https://psmag.com/news/ag-census-finds-more-female-farmers-than-ever, 2020 by The Social Justice Foundation.

Autonomy and meaning are not something you'll find as a corporate assistant in a bigger city where the salary is just enough to pay your rent but have nothing in savings.

Aside from being your own boss or landing a job that you find truly meaningful, think of the financial benefits that come with life in rural America as well. As discussed in Chapter 5, we were able to purchase an amazing house for just $39,000. While that price was exceptional, the inventory of affordable residential real estate throughout rural communities is staggering. The same is true for commercial properties. For example, the vacant, 1950's-era movie theater here in our town was listed at just $25,000 before it sold a couple of years ago. Of course, these properties needed some additional investment and elbow grease. Even so, the result is a finished building that's twice the size of what you find in bigger cities with all the modern updates at half the total investment. In rural communities, even if you were to build something new, permitting and inspections fees are often much lower than in bigger cities as well. Rent is cheaper, taxes are lower, and business startup costs are much more manageable.

These financial factors are perhaps more important for millennials to consider than any other generation. It's widely known that our generation is saddled with more student loan debt than any before. The average millennial's ability to make a "major purchase" is lower than any other generation, according to the 2016 Gallup study, titled: *How Millennials Want to Work and Live*.[7] This means things like financing a wedding, buying a car, buying a house, or even covering the costs of home repairs or a new appliance are out of reach for most. Almost all of those things are more affordable in rural areas. This means rural millennials have the opportunity for a greater quality of life and the ability to save for retirement or to pass on an inheritance than our urban dwelling counterparts. If this inability to make a "major purchase" describes you, then I'd recommend you start now looking into a rural life for yourself.

Though I have sprinkled advice and tips throughout this book, let me finish with a more succinct how-to guide for you to add to it. If you think you're ready to

---

[7]From "How Millennials Want to Work and Live," 2016, *Gallup*, https://www.nwais.org/uploaded/conferences/Business_Officers/2019_BusinessOfficers/Resources/Gallup_How_Millennials_Want_to_Work_and_Live.pdf, 2016 by Gallup, Inc.

make the move to rural America, then here's how I'd recommend you do it.

Begin by narrowing down which region or state you might like to live. It's a wide-open target. Keep in mind there are rural places even in high population states like New York and California. By rural, I am primarily referring to an area with a population of about 50,000 or less. But you'll need to do your own research and consider the type of place that might work best for you. Google local happenings there. Check chamber of commerce websites. Try to find an events calendar or tourism site that will give you a sense of the culture in this new location. Make sure it's a place you could see yourself living before you even think about committing. Then think about the things you "need." Is it important for you to have a Target store or organic farm to table restaurant within thirty minutes? Your future rural community may not have that but the bigger city just a short drive away probably will.

Then, if possible, visit the place. The Airbnb you book in the attractive small town well outside a bigger city will probably be half the price of something you're used to. Visit the local shops, ask locals about fun things to do in town, and drive around neighborhoods to check out homes for sale or rent. Remember, it is common for real estate to be for sale in a small town without ever being posted online. Our home was one example. Keep an eye out for properties with a garage or workshop if you need space to craft products for your own company. Peep in the windows of old commercial buildings that might need a little elbow grease. Downtown revitalizations are happening in towns large and small across this country. Buying that cool old building now could really pay off for you down the road.

There's also about a ninety-nine percent chance that internet connectivity will be important to you, especially if you plan to start your own business. So the next thing I'd recommend you do is research connectivity within the area you plan to live. Many small towns have great internet service, but often you can drive just five miles out of town and there are basically no options. For example, we have excellent service here in Yanceyville. But most of our friends who live elsewhere in Caswell County have very slow DSL, satellite internet, or simply no options at all. We wrongly assumed high speed internet connections were available everywhere before we moved, but we got lucky. Rural America still struggles with connectivity. It is vitally important that you know and plan for that if you decide to move.

Perhaps one of the biggest decisions you'll make if you decide to relocate is about employment. This can be scary, but I firmly believe your opportunities will be greater in rural America than back in the big city. Are you able to keep your current job and work from home or a remote office? If so, you'll want to look into a large enough home with an extra room for an office or a nearby office to rent like the one I found in Danville. Also check to see if your small town has a coworking space. A lot of rural areas have coworking offices now as a way to close the residential internet gap.

Don't forget, the playing field is often wide open if you want to start your own business. If that's your plan, then you'll need to do some research into what your small market lacks. My guess is it lacks quite a bit, especially compared to the convenience and variety you're used to. For example, there were no flower shops in our town. So as soon as Celia started Caswell Flower Company, she instantly became the number one flower farmer and florist in the area. Overnight! She's able to sell her arrangements directly to customers after connecting and transacting online and doesn't even need a brick and mortar shop. You can do that too.

If you do decide to start a new business in your new small town then allow me to offer a word of advice: give the name of your business some sort of local connection. Caswell Flower Company, for example, is pretty obvious and self-explanatory. You need some flowers in or around Caswell County? Who else would you call? More importantly it accomplishes several things. First, it lets folks who were born and raised in our area know that we value and appreciate it as well. Second, it makes the name of the business much easier to remember. Finally, it ensures that an online search using any similar key terms almost always lands the business at the top of the results list.

Perhaps you have the skills to take over and revitalize something that's dying in your small town. Would your marketing degree help you reinvigorate the local chamber of commerce? Would your journalism degree or writing skills help revive the struggling hometown newspaper? Would your social media skills help dozens of "old school" businesses in your area move into the twenty-first century? My guess is they would. Rural America is starved for tech-savvy professionals who—as simple as this sounds—know how the internet works. You just have to think creatively about how the skills you possess can benefit your community.

As you make your move to Small Town, USA., let me give you this final piece of advice: establish meaningful relationships fast. I discussed earlier how important it can be to build local relationships in a professional capacity. This can help you find a job, buy a house, or get appointed to an advisory board for example. However, it's perhaps more important to make quality friendships with people in your age range, which is tough. In any rural area you will quickly notice one thing: the population, on average, is older. Whether you're visiting or moving in, you will probably catch yourself in a moment where you look around and think, "Where are all the people my age?" I asked this same question. Don't worry; they're there. You just have to find your own way of connecting with them. I remember keeping an eye out for folks our age almost everywhere. I'd be in the grocery eyeing couples that looked to be in their thirties as if they were an endangered species and I was on safari.

Our trick was honestly a bit cheesy. Whenever we were out and would strike up a conversation with some potential friends, we'd invite them out to join us for our weekly tradition, Taco Tuesday. Every Tuesday night at our local Mexican restaurant—we only have one in town so it's pretty easy to find—we're there for dollar tacos, discounted beer, and half price margaritas. Who doesn't want to be your friend when there are tacos and beer involved, right? No one we want to be friends with, for sure. We'd meet folks at the local farmer's market and invite them to Taco Tuesday. I had a younger couple come into my office with land records questions. After some conversation, I invited them to Taco Tuesday. I even met a friend while I was in a panic at our bank because we nearly overdrew our honeymoon funds. Taco Tuesday. In fact, the guy I met at the bank that day—now an English teacher—helped me proofread the first draft of this book and took our picture for the cover. He's a great friend.

Putting ourselves out there a little bit in order to establish these friendships was sometimes awkward but it has really paid off. To illustrate, I started this chapter before our daughter Waylen was born, and I'm finishing it now as she's about three weeks old. Yet despite only having been in this community for a few short years, we've had at least two dozen friends and neighbors do things like buy us baby clothes, add money to her college savings account, and even drop off pre-made meals to make life a little easier as we learn the ropes of becoming new parents. Some of these people were perfect strangers just a few months ago.

It's true what they say about small town charm and cohesion, and you will want to get in on that action as soon as possible. Social capital is often more valuable than financial capital and vitally important as you make this leap. I also honestly believe it's the gateway to much more meaningful and fulfilling relationships than those you make in a big, busy city. That has certainly proven to be the case for us.

The truth is people kind of need each other a little more out here in rural America. Without the conveniences of instant delivery or meals at the touch of a phone, you must rely on your neighbors...and they rely on you. The desire to build your community into something meaningful means the bickering of national politics takes a back seat. The striving for new community assets means the entrepreneurs and risk-takers are encouraged. The shared sense of having to push a little bit harder for what you want makes the rewards that much sweeter. That's the life we've found out here in "the middle of nowhere," and I believe it's the life you will find too.

# <u>Appendix of Action</u>

## **CHECKLIST: Moving to the "Middle of Nowhere"**

- ☐ Research states or regions in which you might like to live.

- ☐ If possible, budget a trip to your future rural community to learn more about the place before making the move.

- ☐ Can you take your job with you?

- ☐ If you keep your job during the move, have you planned for what might happen if the terms you established with your boss change?

- ☐ Can you work remotely or work from home?

- ☐ Is your new small town going to have enough of what you "need?" (fitness centers, restaurants, breweries, shops, etc.)

- ☐ Is your small town within reasonable driving distance of a big city, regional airport, hospital, etc.?

- ☐ Have you checked the internet connectivity in your new community?

- ☐ Research festivals and events to get a sense of the culture.

- ☐ If you're religious, is there a church of your denomination?

- ☐ Call the chamber of commerce to ask about local job opportunities that may not be listed online.

## Your Ideas:

_____

_____

_____

_____

_____

_____

_____

_____

## Your To-Do List:

_____

_____

_____

_____

_____

_____

_____

_____

_____

_____

_____

_____

_____

_____

## CHECKLIST: Finding Affordable Places to Rent

☐ Make calls to groups who may know about rental properties not listed online (downtown associations, chambers of commerce, etc.)

☐ Drive around your new community looking for rental signs. (This has the added benefit of giving you a quicker sense of how all the local roads connect).

☐ Consider office rental in the vacant rooms of other businesses like law firms or accounting companies.

☐ Be sure to mention you're looking for rental property to new people you meet. You never know if they themselves might have some available.

☐ Call real estate companies to ask about rental houses even if they only have for sale homes listed on their websites.

☐ Be willing to work from home, if possible, for several months to begin with. As you meet people in your new community, you may be able to use those connections to find affordable rental properties nearby.

☐ Find out if there's a coworking space in your new town or within driving distance before moving in.

## Your Ideas:

_____

_____

_____

_____

_____

_____

_____

## Your To-Do List:

_____

_____

_____

_____

_____

_____

_____

_____

_____

_____

_____

_____

_____

_____

# CHECKLIST: Planning a Wedding on a Budget

- ☐ Do you have talented friends who can provide services?

- ☐ Research and make phone calls to inquire about unconventional wedding venues in the area.

- ☐ Draft a contract, if necessary, to ensure that the property owner agrees to what you have in mind.

- ☐ If your wedding is outdoors, do you have a rain delay date?

- ☐ Give yourself plenty of time to work on your venue if there's never been a wedding there before. (several months at least)

- ☐ Have you established good lines of communication with the owners of the venue? Be sure they feel comfortable with your access to the property when needed.

- ☐ Make lists of decorations and other wedding necessities you may be able to make yourself and not have to buy.

- ☐ If serving alcohol, be sure you have the proper required state or local permitting.

- ☐ If using an unconventional officiant, does your state allow non-religions persons to conduct wedding ceremonies?

- ☐ Think about unconventional food options and how a unique menu may be able to save you money.

- ☐ Is it possible to form a partnership with the property owners after your wedding and turn this into a regular business?

## Your Ideas:

_____

_____

_____

_____

_____

_____

_____

## Your To-Do List:

_____

_____

_____

_____

_____

_____

_____

_____

_____

_____

_____

_____

_____

_____

## CHECKLIST: Getting Involved and Making a Difference

- ☐ Check local government and nonprofit websites to find volunteer opportunities that suit your interests.

- ☐ Be willing to do tasks others don't want to do like take meeting minutes, manual labor, and/or cleaning duties.

- ☐ Look for opportunities on local Facebook pages since many small-town groups will not have an established website.

- ☐ If appropriate, share pictures of your organization's activities on social media to draw more public support.

- ☐ Teach others how to use social media and manage websites in order to help grow their organizations.

- ☐ Attend county commission or town council meetings in order to inform yourself of local current events.

- ☐ Register to vote as soon as you've moved in.

- ☐ Change your phone number to one with your new area code, minimizing the "where are you from?" conversations.

- ☐ Familiarize yourself with important local events that may need volunteers like back-to-school drives, voter registration drives, street cleanups, etc.

- ☐ Contribute, don't command. Though you may bring skills that seem revolutionary to your new community, you must invest time and let others lead in order to earn local trust.

## Your Ideas:

_____

_____

_____

_____

_____

_____

_____

## Your To-Do List:

_____

_____

_____

_____

_____

_____

_____

_____

_____

_____

_____

_____

_____

_____

_____

_____

# CHECKLIST: Buying/Renovating Affordable Real Estate

☐ Has an inspector or estimator viewed the home before you purchased it?

☐ Is the house structurally sound? There's no use buying it if it's beyond repair.

☐ Which local bank will give you the best financing and interest rates?

☐ Does your contractor have the proper state licensing?

☐ Is your contractor insured?

☐ Will you be able to do any of the work yourself?

☐ Has your contractor done projects like yours before?

☐ Ensure that the contractor won't get paid the full amount until the project is finished.

☐ Are there things you can do to assist your contractor and, in turn, save money on the total project costs?

☐ Can you qualify for redevelopment or historic tax credits?

☐ Will the house need asbestos abatement?

☐ Can you afford eco-friendly and sustainable upgrades?

☐ Is the house in a neighborhood where you can see your kids growing up and/or see yourself retiring?

☐ What is the zoning for your property and what are the odds that new development could change the neighborhood?

☐ Grouping your home insurance policy with other insured items like cars may give you cheaper overall rates.

☐ Is there a possibility you could turn a new house into investment property and create monthly rental income?

## Your Ideas:

_____

_____

_____

_____

_____

_____

_____

## Your To-Do List:

_____

_____

_____

_____

_____

_____

_____

_____

_____

_____

_____

_____

_____

_____

_____

## <u>CHECKLIST: Landing a Great New Job</u>

☐ Tailor your resume for each job you're applying for. Talk about how your skills would translate for each job.

☐ Consider starting with an internship or apprenticeship if it will lead to a great job later.

☐ Don't be afraid to apply for jobs you'd like, even if you don't think you're fully qualified for them.

☐ Get involved in your new community as soon as possible. Having close, meaningful relationships with community leaders will help you learn about available jobs sooner.

☐ After getting to know important people in the community, ask to list them as professional references on your resume.

☐ Since you have a lower cost of living now, consider spending some money on new training or certifications that will help you qualify for the jobs you want.

☐ Consider taking a job that may be a step or two below where you'd like to be eventually, then seek a promotion when the time is right.

☐ Create your own job or small business by filling a void in your new local market.

## Your Ideas:

_____

_____

_____

_____

_____

_____

_____

## Your To-Do List:

_____

_____

_____

_____

_____

_____

_____

_____

_____

_____

_____

_____

_____

# CHECKLIST: Building A Meaningful Life

- ☐ Ensure your new move and lifestyle will save you money.

- ☐ Use that saved money to pay off debt or finance memorable trips to interesting places.

- ☐ Make a list of things to do or places to visit where you might find new friends your age.

- ☐ Take the initiative to introduce yourself to your new neighbors and get to know them personally.

- ☐ Offer to help elderly neighbors with difficult tasks.

- ☐ If you have kids, do some research on the quality of nearby public, charter, or private schools.

- ☐ Do some market research into what businesses or products your new community lacks.

- ☐ Determine the feasibility of starting your own new business to fill that market void.

- ☐ Make a point to purposefully thank those who help you, even if their help was a small gesture.

- ☐ Think about ways in which your job or volunteer activities can have a positive impact on your community.

- ☐ Once you've established new friends, invite them over frequently for dinner parties, game days, birthdays, etc.

- ☐ Get to know your new town's history and unique attributes.

- ☐ Think about what you enjoyed about life in a bigger city, like trivia night or run clubs, then initiate it in your new town.

- ☐ Buy local.

## Your Ideas:

_____

_____

_____

_____

_____

_____

_____

## Your To-Do List:

_____

_____

_____

_____

_____

_____

_____

_____

_____

_____

_____

_____

_____